I0797714

HISTORY OF
FOOTBALL

KENNY ABDO

Fly!
An Imprint of Abdo Zoom
abdobooks.com

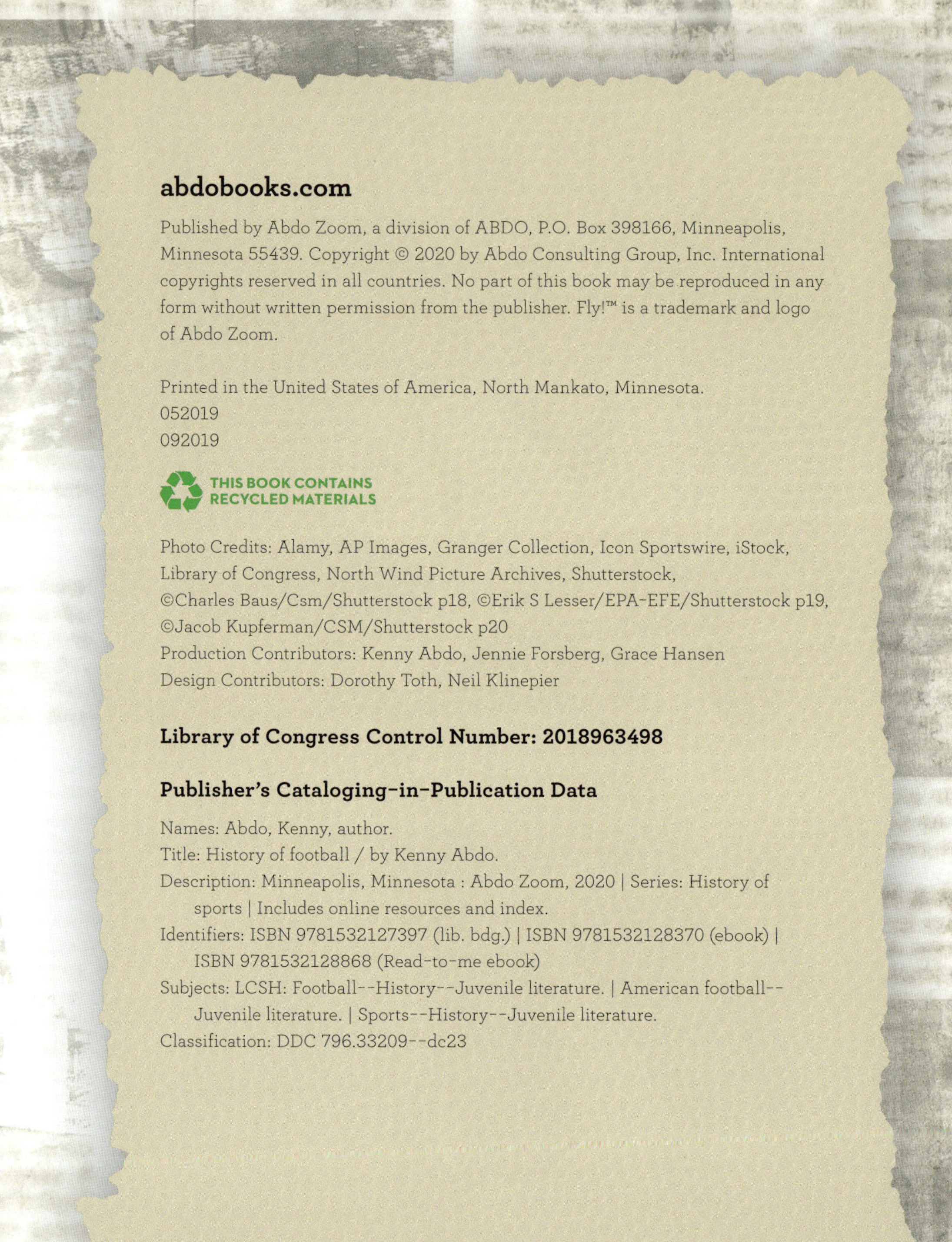

abdobooks.com

Published by Abdo Zoom, a division of ABDO, P.O. Box 398166, Minneapolis, Minnesota 55439.

Printed in the United States of America, North Mankato, Minnesota.
052019
092019

THIS BOOK CONTAINS RECYCLED MATERIALS

Photo Credits: Alamy, AP Images, Granger Collection, Icon Sportswire, iStock, Library of Congress, North Wind Picture Archives, Shutterstock, ©Charles Baus/Csm/Shutterstock p18, ©Erik S Lesser/EPA-EFE/Shutterstock p19, ©Jacob Kupferman/CSM/Shutterstock p20
Production Contributors: Kenny Abdo, Jennie Forsberg, Grace Hansen
Design Contributors: Dorothy Toth, Neil Klinepier

Library of Congress Control Number: 2018963498

Publisher's Cataloging-in-Publication Data

Names: Abdo, Kenny, author.
Title: History of football / by Kenny Abdo.
Description: Minneapolis, Minnesota : Abdo Zoom, 2020 | Series: History of sports | Includes online resources and index.
Identifiers: ISBN 9781532127397 (lib. bdg.) | ISBN 9781532128370 (ebook) | ISBN 9781532128868 (Read-to-me ebook)
Subjects: LCSH: Football--History--Juvenile literature. | American football--Juvenile literature. | Sports--History--Juvenile literature.
Classification: DDC 796.33209--dc23

TABLE OF CONTENTS

FOOTBALL

Football scores big with fans from college games to pro bowls to fantasy **leagues**. With hundreds of years of history, the sport is one of the most popular in the world.

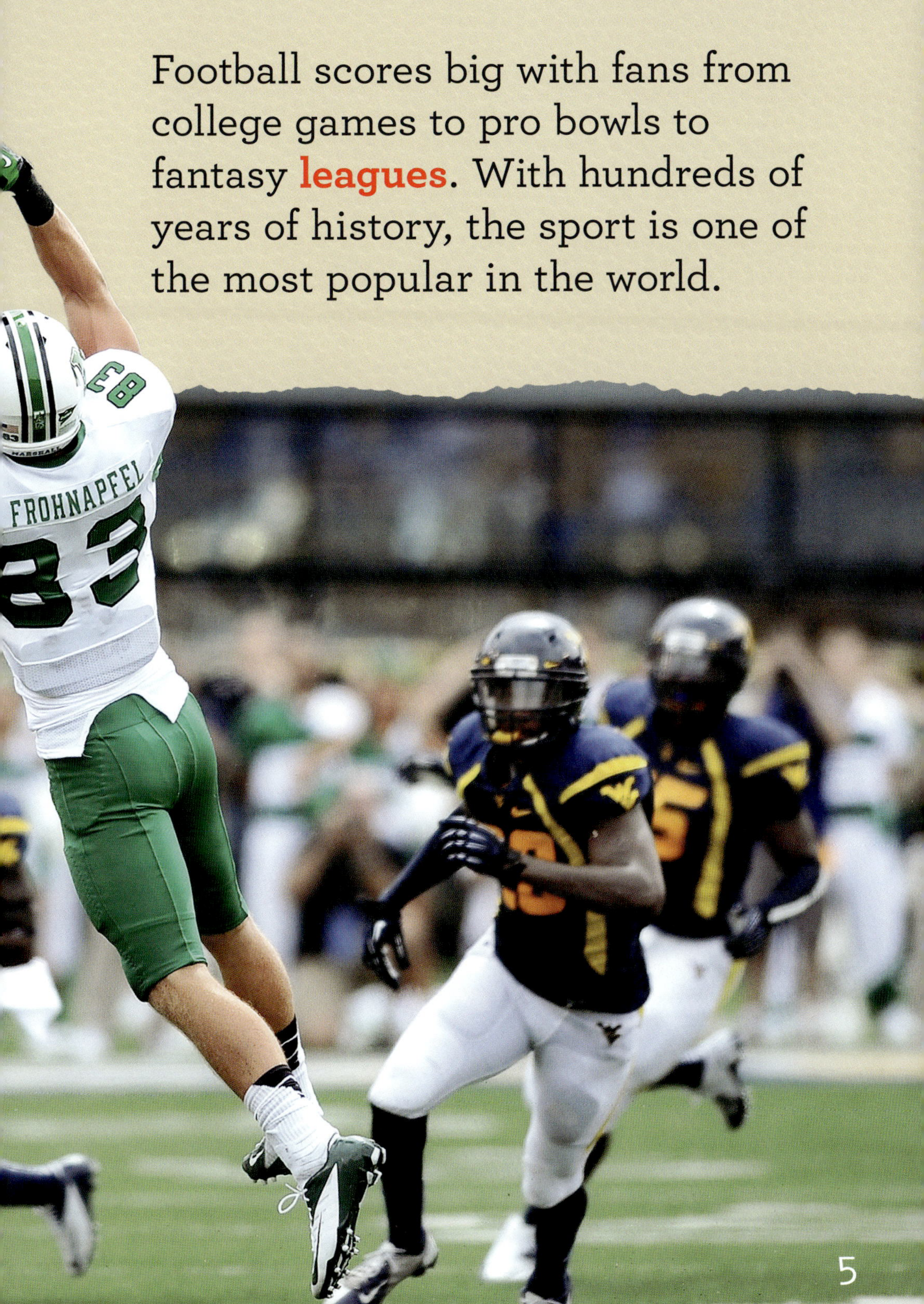

Football is played between two teams of 11 players. They play on a 100-yard long field that has goalposts on each end. Each team can score points in many ways. One team getting the ball into the other team's **end zone** is the main goal.

WARM UP

Football is believed to come from the English games **rugby** and soccer. American football was started by player and coach Walter Camp from Yale University.

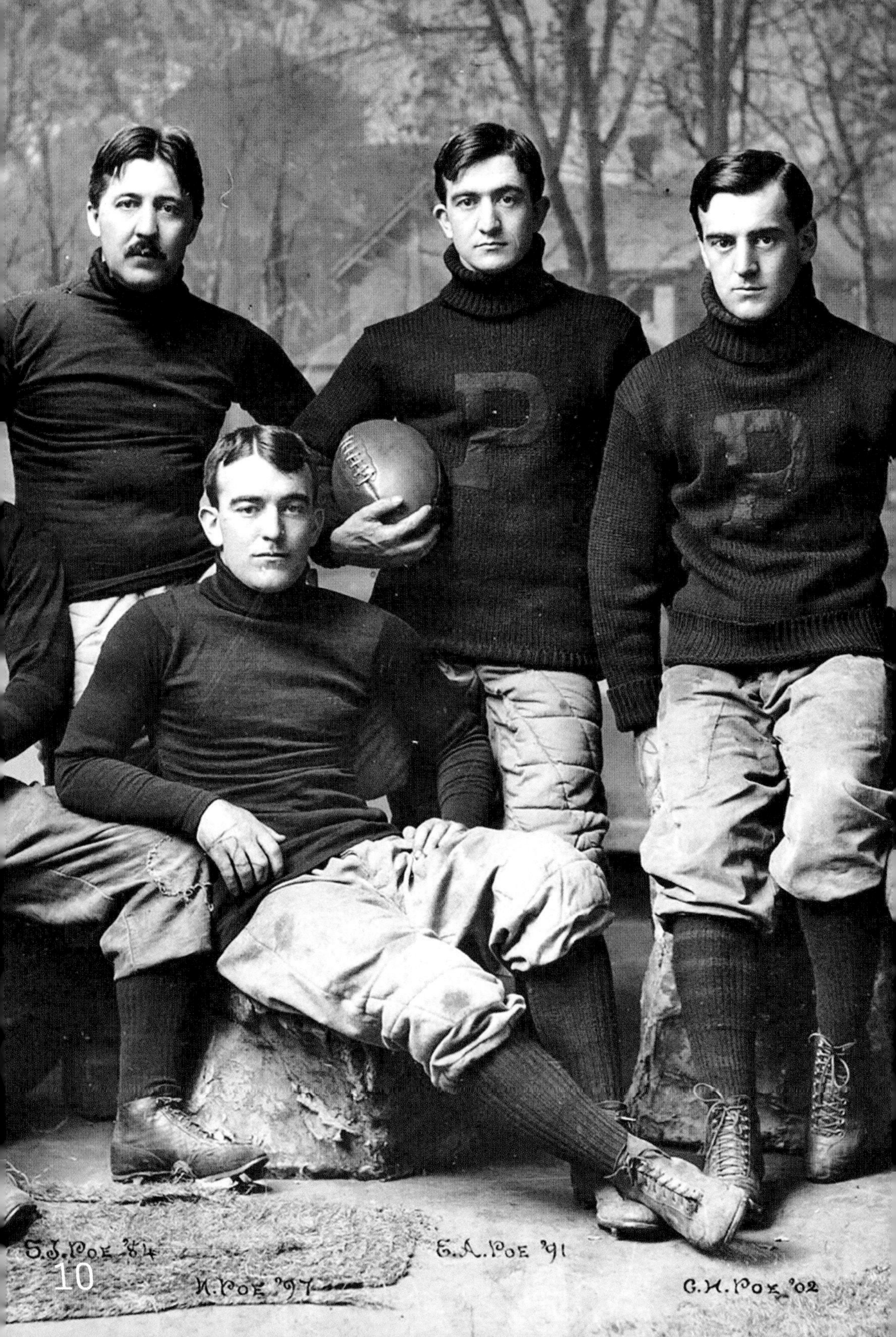
S.J. Poe '84
E.A. Poe '91
N. Poe '97
G.H. Poe '02

The first game of football was played in 1869. Princeton University went up against Rutgers University. The rules were more like **rugby's** and the ball was round. Rutgers won the game, 6 to 4.

The National Football **League** (NFL) was created in 1920. The American Football League (AFL) was created 40 years later.

In 1967, the NFL and AFL decided to play against each other. It was called the AFL–NFL **Championship** Game or the **Super Bowl**.

In 1970, the AFL joined the NFL forming one **league**. Today, the **Super Bowl** is still played between the National Football Conference (NFC) and the American Football Conference (AFC).

The winning team of the **Super Bowl** gets the Vince Lombardi **trophy**. It is made of sterling silver and is valued at more than $25,000!

BIG SHOW

Washington Redskins quarterback Frank Filchock set a record in 1939. He threw a 99-yard pass to fullback Andy Farkas for a touchdown. Eli Manning matched the feat by tossing a 99-yard **bomb** to Victor Cruz in 2011.

In 2018, the Philadelphia Eagles beat the New England Patriots at **Super Bowl** LII. Eagles quarterback Nick Foles, who passed for 373 yards and three touchdowns, **clinched** the Most Valuable Player (MVP) award. He is the first player to ever throw and catch a touchdown pass at a Super Bowl!

TROPHY
NFL
AFC vs NFC

PATRIOTS
12
58
WHITE
28

Tom Brady is considered one of the best players in NFL history. He has led the Patriots to the **Super Bowl** nine times! They beat the LA Rams in 2019, making it their sixth **championship** victory!

GLOSSARY

bomb – a long pass thrown to a receiver.

championship – a game held to find a first-place winner.

clinch – to confirm a win.

end zone – the area at the end of the field that the ball must enter to score a touchdown.

league – a group of teams that compete against each other.

rugby – a game played between two teams of 13 players. The ball can be kicked, carried, and passed from hand to hand to score a goal. Forward passing is not allowed.

Super Bowl – the NFL championship game played once a year.

trophy – an object you receive as a prize for winning during a game or event.

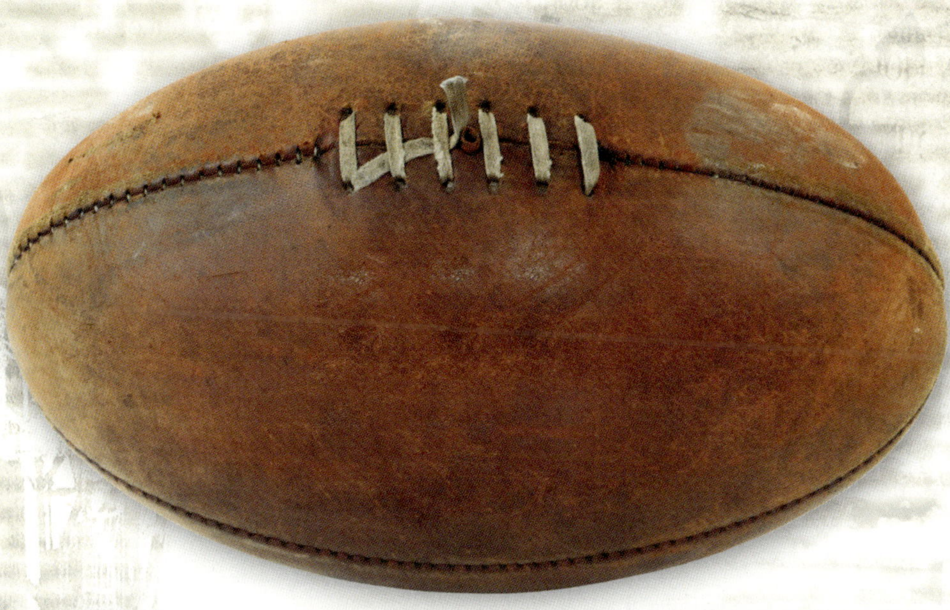

ONLINE RESOURCES

To learn more about football, please visit **abdobooklinks.com** or scan this QR code. These links are routinely monitored and updated to provide the most current information available.

INDEX